Table of Co

CW00503871

- **Identity, governance, privacy, and compliance features**
  - Secure access to your applications by using Azure identity services
  - Build a cloud governance strategy on Azure
  - Examine privacy, compliance, and data protection standards on Azure
- **Azure cost management and service level agreements**
  - Plan and manage your Azure costs
  - Choose the right Azure services by examining SLAs and service lifecycle

Cloud Concepts

Introduction to Azure Fundamentals

What is cloud computing?

- It's the delivery of computing services over the internet, which is otherwise known as the cloud.
- These services include servers, storage, databases, networking, software, analytics, and intelligence.
- Cloud computing offers faster innovation, flexible resources, and economies of scale.

Why is cloud computing typically cheaper to use?

- You typically pay only for the cloud services you use, which helps you:
    - Lower your operating costs.
    - Run your infrastructure more efficiently.
    - Scale as your business needs change.
- You can treat cloud resources like you would your resources in your own datacenter. When you're done using them, you give them back. You're billed only for what you use.
- Instead of maintaining CPUs and storage in your datacenter, you rent them for the time that you need them.
- The cloud provider takes care of maintaining the underlying infrastructure for you.

Why should I move to the cloud?

- To power your services and deliver innovative and novel user experiences more quickly, the cloud provides on-demand access to.

- A nearly limitless pool of raw compute, storage, and networking components.
- Speech recognition and other cognitive services that help make your application stand out from the crowd.
- Analytics services that deliver telemetry data from your software and devices.

What are some cloud computing advantages?

- There are several benefits that a cloud environment has over a physical environment.
    - **Reliability:** Continuous user experience with no apparent downtime even when things go wrong.
    - **Elasticity**: Cloud-based applications can be configured to always have the resources they need. You can configure cloud-based apps to take advantage of autoscaling, so your apps always have the resources they need.
    - **Agility**: Cloud-based resources can be deployed and configured quickly as your application requirements change.
    - **Scalability:**
        - *Vertically*: Computing capacity can be increased by adding RAM or CPUs to a virtual machine.
        - *Horizontally*: Computing capacity can be increased by adding instances of a resource, such as adding more virtual machines to your configuration.
    - **Geo-distribution**: Applications and data can be deployed to regional datacenters around the globe,

so your customers always have the best performance in their region.

- ○ **Disaster recovery**: By taking advantage of cloud-based backup services, data replication, and geo-distribution, you can deploy your applications with the confidence that comes from knowing that your data is safe if disaster should occur

What are cloud service models?

- Cloud computing falls into one of the following computing models. These models define the different levels of shared responsibility that a cloud provider and cloud tenant are responsible for.
- **PaaS**
  - ○ Platform as a service refers to cloud computing services that supply an on-demand environment for developing, testing, delivering, and managing software applications.
  - ○ PaaS is designed to make it easier for developers to quickly create web or mobile apps, without worrying about setting up or managing the underlying infrastructure of servers, storage, network, and databases needed for development.
- **SaaS**
  - ○ Software as a service is a method for delivering software applications over the Internet, on demand and typically on a subscription basis.
  - ○ With SaaS, cloud service providers host and manage the software application and underlying infrastructure.

- These providers also handle any maintenance, such as software upgrades and security patching.
- Users connect to the application over the Internet, usually with a web browser on their phone, tablet, or PC.

- **IaaS**
  - Infrastructure as a service (IaaS) is a type of cloud computing service that offers essential compute, storage, and networking resources on demand, on a pay-as-you-go basis.
  - This cloud service model is the closest to managing physical servers.
  - A cloud provider keeps the hardware up to date, but operating system maintenance and network configuration is left to the cloud tenant.
  - IaaS lets you bypass the cost and complexity of buying and managing physical servers and data centre infrastructure

	You Manage	Cloud Provider Manages	
On-premises (Private Cloud)	Infrastructure (as a Service)	Platform (as a Service)	Software (as a Service)
Data & Access	Data & Access	Data & Access	Data & Access
Applications	Applications	Applications	Applications
Runtime	Runtime	Runtime	Runtime
Operating System	Operating System	Operating System	Operating System
Virtual Machine	Virtual Machine	Virtual Machine	Virtual Machine
Compute	Compute	Compute	Compute
Networking	Networking	Networking	Networking
Storage	Storage	Storage	Storage

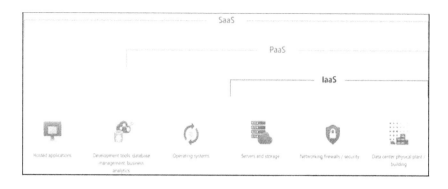

PaaS	Azure SQL Database, Azure SQL Managed Instance, Azure App Service, Azure Cosmo DB, Azure Synapse Analytics
IaaS	SQL Server on Azure VM, Azure Virtual Machine, Azure Storage Account

What is Azure?

- Azure is a continually expanding set of cloud services that help your organization meet your current and future business challenges.
- Azure gives you the freedom to build, manage, and deploy applications on a massive global network using your favorite tools and frameworks.

What does Azure offer?

- Be ready for the future.
- Build on your terms.
- Operate hybrid seamlessly.
- Trust your cloud

What can I do with Azure?

- Azure provides more than 100 services that enable you to do everything from running your existing applications on virtual machines.
- Azure provides AI and machine-learning services that can naturally communicate with your users through vision, hearing, and speech.
- It also provides storage solutions that dynamically grow to accommodate massive amounts of data.
- Azure services enable solutions that aren't feasible without the power of the cloud.

What is the Azure portal?

- The Azure portal is a web-based, unified console that provides an alternative to command-line tools.
- With the Azure portal, you can manage your Azure subscription by using a graphical user interface.
- The Azure portal is designed for resiliency and continuous availability.
- It maintains a presence in every Azure datacenter.
- The Azure portal updates continuously and requires no downtime for maintenance activities.
- You can:
  - Build, manage, and monitor everything from simple web apps to complex cloud deployments.
  - Create custom dashboards for an organized view of resources.
  - Configure accessibility options for an optimal experience.

What is Azure Marketplace?

- It helps connect users with Microsoft partners, independent software vendors, and startups that are offering their solutions and services, which are optimized to run on Azure.
- Azure Marketplace customers can find, try, purchase, and provision applications and services from hundreds of leading service providers.
- All solutions and services are certified to run on Azure.
- Using Azure Marketplace, you can provision end-to-end solutions quickly and reliably, hosted in your own Azure environment.
- Azure Marketplace is designed for IT pros and cloud developers interested in commercial and IT software.

<u>Content of this link help you in exam for match making</u> **(You can get at least 2-3 matchmaking question based on different azure services and their work so this link has summary of all azure service)**
https://docs.microsoft.com/en-gb/learn/modules/intro-to-azure-fundamentals/tour-of-azure-services

Azure accounts

- To create and use Azure services, you need an Azure subscription.
- You can purchase Azure access directly from Microsoft by signing up on the Azure website or through a Microsoft representative.
- You can also purchase Azure access through a Microsoft partner.
- The **Azure free account** includes:

- o   Free access to popular Azure products for 12 months.
  - o   A credit to spend for the **first 30 days**.
  - o   Access to **more than 25 products** that are always free.
- The **Azure free student account** offer includes:
  - o   Free access to certain Azure services for 12 months.
  - o   A credit to use in the **first 12 months**.
  - o   Free access to **certain software developer tools**.
  - o   The Azure free student account is an offer for students that gives $100 credit and free developer tools. Also, you can sign up **without a credit card**

Discuss Azure Fundamental Concepts

What is serverless computing?

- In understanding the definition of serverless computing, it's important to note that servers are still running the code.
- The serverless name comes from the fact that the tasks associated with infrastructure provisioning and management are invisible to the developer.
- This approach enables developers to increase their focus on the business logic and deliver more value to the core of the business.
- Serverless computing helps teams increase their productivity and bring products to market faster.
- It allows organizations to better optimize resources and stay focused on innovation.

What are public, private, and hybrid clouds?

- There are three deployment models for cloud computing: *public cloud*, *private cloud*, and *hybrid cloud*. Each deployment model has different aspects that you should consider as you migrate to the cloud.

Deployment model	Description
Public cloud	Services are offered over the public internet and available to anyone who wants to purchase them. Cloud resources like servers and storage are owned and operated by a third-party cloud service provider and delivered over the internet.

Private cloud	Computing resources are used exclusively by users from one business or organization. A private cloud can be physically located at your organization's on-site datacenter. It also can be hosted by a third-party service provider.
Hybrid cloud	This computing environment combines a public cloud and a private cloud by allowing data and applications to be shared between them.

- **Public cloud**
  - No capital expenditures to scale up.
  - Applications can be quickly provisioned and deprovisioned.
  - Organizations pay only for what they use.

- **Private cloud**
  - Hardware must be purchased for start-up and maintenance.
  - Organizations have complete control over resources and security.
  - Organizations are responsible for hardware maintenance and updates.

- **Hybrid cloud**
  - Provides the most flexibility.
  - Organizations determine where to run their applications.
  - Organizations control security, compliance, or legal requirements.

- **Capital expenses vs. operating expenses**
  - **CapEx** requires significant up-front financial costs, as well as ongoing maintenance and support

expenditures. By contrast, **OpEx** is a consumption-based model.

- ○ **Capital Expenditure (CapEx)**
  - ■ It is the **up-front spending** of money on physical infrastructure, and then deducting that up-front expense over time.
  - ■ The up-front cost from CapEx has a **value that reduces over time.**
- ○ **Operational Expenditure (OpEx)**
  - ■ It is spending money on services or products now and **being billed** for them now.
  - ■ You can deduct this expense in the same year you spend it.
  - ■ There is **no up-front cost**, as you **pay for a service or product as you use it.**
- ○ A consumption-based model has many benefits, including:
  - ■ No upfront costs.
  - ■ No need to purchase and manage costly infrastructure that users might not use to its fullest.
  - ■ The ability to pay for additional resources when they are needed.
  - ■ The ability to stop paying for resources that are no longer needed.

Core Azure Architectural Components

- **Subscriptions**:
    - A subscription groups together user accounts and the resources that have been created by those user accounts.
    - For each subscription, there are limits or quotas on the number of resources that you can create and use.
    - Organizations can use subscriptions to manage costs and the resources that are created by users, teams, or projects. Subscription is a logical unit of Azure.

- **Management groups**
    - These groups help you manage access, policy, and compliance for multiple subscriptions.
    - All subscriptions in a management group automatically inherit the conditions applied to the management group.

- **Azure regions**
    - A *region* is a geographical area on the planet that contains **at least one but potentially multiple datacenters** that are nearby and networked together with a low-latency network.
    - Azure intelligently assigns and controls the resources within each region to ensure workloads are appropriately balanced.

- These regions give you the flexibility to bring applications closer to your users no matter where they are.
- Global regions provide better scalability and redundancy.
- They also preserve data residency for your services.
- There are also some global Azure services that **don't require you to select a particular region**, such as *Azure Active Directory, Azure Traffic Manager, and Azure DNS.*
- Some services or VM features are only available in certain regions.
- Regions are what you use to identify the location for your resources.

- **Special Azure regions**
  - Azure has specialized regions that you might want to use when you build out your applications for compliance or legal purposes. A few examples include:
    - **US DoD Central, US Gov Virginia, US Gov Iowa and more:**
      - These regions are physical and logical network-isolated instances of Azure for U.S. government agencies and partners.
      - These datacenters are *operated by screened U.S. personnel and include additional compliance certifications.*
    - **China East, China North, and more:**
      - These regions are available through a unique partnership between Microsoft

and 21Vianet, **whereby Microsoft doesn't directly maintain** the datacenters.

- **Azure Availability Zone**
    - Availability zones are physically separate datacenters within an Azure region.
    - Each availability zone is made up of **one or more datacenters** equipped with **independent power, cooling, and networking**.
    - An availability zone is set up to be an *isolation boundary*.
    - **Not every region** has support for **availability zones**.
    - Availability zones are primarily for *VMs, managed disks, load balancers, and SQL databases*.
    - Availability zones are connected through high-speed, private fiber-optic networks.
    - There's a minimum of three zones within a single region.
    - Azure services that support availability zones fall into two categories:
        - **Zonal services**
        - **Zone-redundant services**

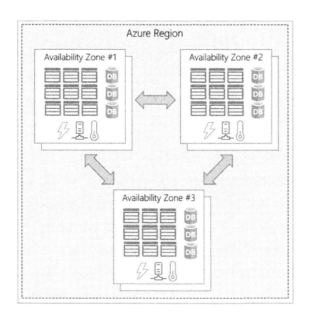

- **Region pair**
    - Each Azure region is always paired with another region within the same geography (such as US, Europe, or Asia) at least 300 miles away.
    - If a region in a pair was affected by a natural disaster, for instance, services would automatically failover to the other region in its region pair.
    - The pair of regions is directly connected and far enough apart to be isolated from regional disasters, you can use them to provide reliable services and data redundancy.
    - Planned Azure updates are rolled out to paired regions one region at a time to minimize downtime and risk of application outage.
    - Data continues to reside within the same geography as its pair (except for Brazil South) for tax- and law-enforcement jurisdiction purposes.

- **Resource**
  - A manageable item that's available through Azure. Virtual machines (VMs), storage accounts, web apps, databases, and virtual networks are examples of resources.

- **Resource Group:**
  - A **folder structure in Azure** in which you organize resources like databases, virtual machines, virtual networks, or almost any resource.
  - All the resources in your resource group should **share the same lifecycle**. You deploy, update, and delete them together. If one resource, such as a server, needs to exist on a different deployment cycle it should be in another resource group.
  - Each **resource can exist in only one resource group.**
  - The resources in a resource group **can be in different regions than the resource group.**
  - A resource group can be used to **scope access control for administrative actions**.
  - To manage a resource group, you can assign Azure Policies, Azure roles, or resource locks.
  - Resource groups are also a scope for applying role-based access control (RBAC) permissions.
  - You can apply tags to a resource group. The resources in the **resource group don't inherit those tags.**
  - A *resource can connect to resources in other resource groups*.
  - To create a resource group, you can use the portal, PowerShell, Azure CLI, or an ARM template

- Some resources can exist outside of a resource group. These resources are deployed to the *subscription, management group, or tenant.*

- **Azure Resource Manager**
  - Azure Resource Manager is the deployment and management service for Azure.
  - It provides a management layer that enables you to create, update, and delete resources in your Azure account.
  - You use management features like access control, locks, and tags to secure and organize your resources after deployment.
  - Benefits of using Resource Manager
  - Manage your infrastructure through declarative templates rather than scripts.
  - Define the dependencies between resources so they're deployed in the correct order.
  - Deploy, manage, and monitor all the resources for your solution as a group, rather than handling these resources individually.
  - Apply access control to all services because RBAC is natively integrated into the management platform.
  - Apply tags to resources to logically organize all the resources in your subscription.
  - Clarify your organization's billing by viewing costs for a group of resources that share the same tag.

- **Azure subscriptions**
  - Using Azure requires an Azure subscription.
  - A subscription provides you with authenticated and authorized access to Azure products and services.

- An Azure subscription is **a logical unit of Azure services** that links to an Azure account, which is an identity in Azure Active Directory (Azure AD) or in a directory that Azure AD trusts.
- An account can have one subscription or multiple subscriptions that have different billing models and to which you apply different access-management policies.
- Subscriptions are bound to some **hard limitations**. For example, the maximum number of Azure ExpressRoute circuits per subscription is 10.
- You can use Azure subscriptions to define boundaries around Azure products, services, and resources.
- There are two types of subscription boundaries that you can use:
  - **Billing boundary**: This subscription type determines how an Azure account is billed for using Azure. You can create multiple subscriptions for different types of billing requirements.
  - **Access control boundary**: Azure applies access-management policies at the subscription level, and you can create separate subscriptions to reflect different organizational structure
- Depending on your needs, you can set up **multiple invoices within the same billing** account.

- **Azure management groups**
  - Azure management groups provide a level of scope above subscriptions.

- You organize subscriptions into containers called management groups and apply your governance conditions to the management groups.
- All subscriptions within a management group automatically inherit the conditions applied to the management group.
- All subscriptions within a single management group must trust the same Azure AD tenant.
- Each management group and subscription can support only one parent.
- Each management group can have many children.
- 10,000 management groups can be supported in a single directory.
- A management group tree can support up to six levels of depth.

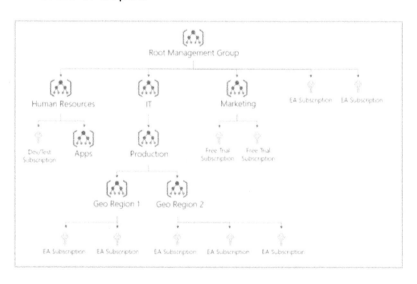

Core Azure services

Azure Compute Services

- Azure compute is an on-demand computing service for running cloud-based applications.
- It provides computing resources such as disks, processors, memory, networking, and operating systems.
- Azure supports a wide range of computing solutions for development and testing, running applications, and extending your datacenter.
- The service supports Linux, Windows Server, SQL Server, Oracle, IBM, and SAP.
- Some of the most prominent services are:
  - Azure Virtual Machines
  - Azure Container Instances
  - Azure App Service
  - Azure Functions (or *serverless computing*)
- Serverless computing includes the abstraction of servers, an event-driven scale, and micro-billing. Azure has two implementations of serverless compute:
  - **Azure Functions**: Functions can execute code in almost any modern language.
  - **Azure Logic Apps**: Logic apps are designed in a web-based designer and can execute logic triggered by Azure services without writing any code.

- **Virtual machines**
  - Virtual machines are software emulations of physical computers.
  - VMs are also an excellent choice when you move from a physical server to the cloud
  - They include a virtual processor, memory, storage, and networking resources.

- VMs host an operating system, and you can install and run software just like a physical computer.
- **When to use**: Use Virtual Machines when you want full control over your application infrastructure or to migrate on-premises application workloads to Azure without having to make changes.
- With Azure Virtual Machines, you can create and use VMs in the cloud.
- Virtual Machines provide infrastructure as a service (IaaS) and can be used in different ways.
- VMs are an ideal choice when you need:
    - Total control over the operating system (OS).
    - The ability to run custom software.
    - To use custom hosting configurations.

- **Virtual machine scale sets**
    - Azure virtual machine scale sets let you create and manage a group of load balanced VMs.
    - Virtual machine scale sets let you deploy and manage a set of **identical virtual machines.**
    - With all VMs configured the same, virtual machine scale sets are designed to support true auto scale. No pre-provisioning of VMs is required.
    - The process of adding or removing VMs can be manual, automated, or a combination of both.
    - Scale sets allow you to centrally manage, configure, and update many VMs in minutes to provide highly available applications.
    - The number of VM instances can **automatically increase or decrease in response to demand** or a defined schedule.

- **Containers and Kubernetes**
  - Container Instances and Azure Kubernetes Service are Azure compute resources that you can use to deploy and manage containers.
  - **Azur Container instance** is a platform as a service (PaaS) offering that allows you to upload your containers, which it runs for you.
  - Containers are lightweight, virtualized application environments.
  - They're designed to be quickly created, scaled out, and stopped dynamically.
  - You can run multiple instances of a containerized application on a single host machine.
  - The task of automating, managing, and interacting with many containers is known as **orchestration**.
  - **Azure Kubernetes Service** is a complete orchestration service for containers with distributed architectures and large volumes of containers.
  - Containers are often used to create solutions by using a *microservice architecture*. This architecture is where you break solutions into smaller, independent pieces.
  - **When to use**: When you need to build production-ready, scalable environments that provide additional scheduling and management tools, or when you're deploying a Docker Swarm cluster

- **App Service**
  - With Azure App Service, you can quickly build, deploy, and scale enterprise-grade web, mobile, and API apps running on any platform.

- Azure App Service is an HTTP-based service for hosting web applications, REST APIs, and mobile back ends.
- You can meet rigorous performance, scalability, security, and compliance requirements while using a fully managed platform to perform infrastructure maintenance.
- App Service is a platform as a service (PaaS) offering.
- App Service on Linux is not supported on the Shared pricing tier.
- App Service handles most of the infrastructure decisions you deal with in hosting web-accessible apps:
  - Deployment and management are integrated into the platform
  - Endpoints can be secured.
  - Sites can be scaled quickly to handle high traffic loads.
  - The built-in load balancing and traffic manager provide high availability.

- **Azure Batch**
  - Azure Batch enables large-scale parallel and high-performance computing (HPC) batch jobs with the ability to scale to tens, hundreds, or thousands of VMs.
  - When you're ready to run a job, Batch does the following:
    - Starts a pool of compute VMs for you.
    - Installs applications and staging data.
    - Run jobs with as many tasks as you have.

- Identifies failures.
- Requeues work.
- Scales down the pool as work completes.

- **Functions**
  - Functions are ideal when you're concerned only about the **code running** your service and **not the underlying platform** or infrastructure.
  - Functions can be either stateless or stateful.
  - Functions are a key component of serverless computing.
  - They're commonly used when you need to perform **work in response to an event** (often via a REST request), timer, or message from another Azure service, and when that work can be completed quickly, within seconds or less.
  - **When to use**: Use Azure Functions when you have code that is triggered by other Azure services, by web-based events, or on a schedule. You can also use Functions when you don't need the overhead of a complete hosted project or when you only want to pay for the time that your code runs.

- **Logic App**
  - Logic apps are like functions. Both enable you to trigger logic based on an event.
  - Where functions execute code, logic apps execute *workflows* that are designed to automate business scenarios and are built from predefined logic blocks.

- Each time the trigger fires, the Logic Apps engine creates a logic app instance that runs the actions in the workflow.
- **Functions vs. Logic Apps**
  - Functions and Logic Apps can both create complex orchestrations. An orchestration is a collection of functions or steps that are executed to accomplish a complex task.
  - With Functions, you write code to complete each step.
  - With Logic Apps, you use a GUI to define the actions and how they relate to one another.

	Functions	Logic Apps
State	Normally stateless, but Durable Functions provide state.	Stateful
Development	Code-first (imperative).	Designer-first (declarative)
Connectivity	About a dozen built-in binding types. Write code for custom bindings	Large collection of connectors. Enterprise Integration Pack for B2B scenarios. Build custom connectors.
Actions	Each activity is an Azure function. Write code for activity functions	Large collection of ready-made actions

Monitoring	Azure Application Insights	Azure portal, Log Analytics
Management	REST API, Visual Studio	Azure portal, REST API, PowerShell, Visual Studio
Execution context	Can run locally or in the cloud	Runs only in the cloud.

- **Virtual Desktop**
  - Azure Virtual Desktop is a desktop and application virtualization service that runs on the cloud.
  - It enables your users to use a cloud-hosted version of Windows from any location.
  - User sign-in to Azure Virtual Desktop is fast because user profiles are containerized by using FSLogix.
  - Azure Virtual Desktop provides centralized security management for users' desktops with Azure Active Directory (Azure AD).
  - Azure Virtual Desktop uses Azure Monitor for monitoring and alerts.
  - Azure Virtual Desktop lets you use Windows 10 Enterprise multi-session, the only Windows client-based operating system that enables multiple concurrent users on a single VM.
  - Azure Virtual Desktop works across devices like Windows, Mac, iOS, Android, and Linux.

- **How can you reduce costs with Azure Virtual Desktop?**
  - **Bring your own licenses**
    - Bring your eligible Windows or Microsoft 365 license to get Windows 10 Enterprise and

Windows 7 Enterprise desktops and apps at no additional cost.

- If you're an eligible Microsoft Remote Desktop Services Client Access License customer, Windows Server Remote Desktop Services desktops and apps are available at no additional cost.

○ **Save on compute costs**

- Buy one-year or three-year **Azure Reserved Virtual Machine Instances** to save you up to 72 percent versus pay-as-you-go pricing.

- You can pay for a reservation up front or monthly. Reservations provide a billing discount and don't affect the runtime state of your resources.

Explore Azure networking services

- **What is Azure virtual networking**
  - Azure Virtual Network (VNet) is the fundamental building block for your private network in Azure.
  - *Azure virtual networks* enable Azure resources, such as VMs, web apps, and databases, to **communicate with each other,** with users on the internet, and with your on-premises client computers.
  - Azure network as a set of resources that links other Azure resources.
  - All resources in a VNet can communicate outbound to the internet, by default.
  - Azure virtual networks provide the following key networking capabilities:
    - Isolation and segmentation
    - Internet communications
    - Communicate between Azure resources
    - Communicate with on-premises resources
    - Route network traffic
    - Filter network traffic
    - Connect virtual networks
  - Virtual network peering can be used to link virtual networks
  - You also can configure the virtual network to use either an internal or an external DNS server.
  - Azure resources to communicate securely with each other. You can do that in one of two ways:

- **Virtual networks** Virtual networks can connect not only VMs but other Azure resources
- **Service endpoints** You can use service endpoints to connect to other Azure resource types,
- There are three mechanisms for you to achieve Communicate with on-premises resources connectivity:
  - **Point-to-site virtual private networks**: The typical approach to a virtual private network (VPN) connection is from a computer outside your organization, back into your corporate network.
  - **Site-to-site virtual private networks:** A site-to-site VPN links your on-premises VPN device or gateway to the Azure VPN gateway in a virtual network.
  - **Azure ExpressRoute:** where you need greater bandwidth and even higher levels of security
- By default, Azure routes traffic between subnets on any connected virtual networks, on-premises networks, and the internet
- You also can control routing and override those settings, as follows:
  - **Route tables:** A route table allows you to define rules about how traffic should be directed. You can create custom route tables with routes that control where traffic is routed to for each subnet.

- **Border Gateway Protocol** Border Gateway Protocol (BGP) works with Azure VPN gateways or ExpressRoute
  - Azure virtual networks enable you to filter traffic between subnets by using the following approaches:
    - **Network security groups:** contain multiple inbound and outbound security rules
    - **Network virtual appliances:** A network virtual appliance is a VM that performs a network function, such as a firewall, WAN optimization, or other network function.
  - You can link virtual networks together by using **virtual network *peering*.** Peering enables resources in each virtual network to communicate with each other.
  - UDR is user-defined Routing. UDR is a significant update to Azure's Virtual Networks as this allows network admins to control the routing tables.
  - You create custom routes by either creating user-defined routes, or by exchanging border gateway protocol (BGP) routes between your on-premises network gateway and an Azure virtual network gateway.

- **Azure VPN Gateway**
  - A VPN gateway is a specific type of **virtual network gateway** that is used to **send encrypted traffic** between an Azure virtual network and an on-premises location over the public Internet.

- Azure VPN Gateway instances are deployed in Azure Virtual Network instances and enable the following connectivity:
  - site-to-site connection
  - point-to-site connection
  - network-to-network connection.
- You can deploy only one VPN gateway in each virtual network.
- But you can use one gateway to connect to multiple locations.
- One virtual network can connect to another virtual network in the same region, or in a different Azure region.
- When you deploy a VPN gateway, you specify the VPN type: either *policy-based* or *route-based*.
- The main difference between these two types of VPNs is how traffic to be encrypted is specified.
- In Azure, both types of VPN gateways use a pre-shared key as the only method of authentication.
- Both types also rely on Internet Key Exchange (IKE) in either version 1 or version 2 and Internet Protocol Security (IPSec).
- Policy-based VPN gateways specify statically the IP address of packets that should be encrypted through each tunnel.
  - Support for IKEv1 only.
  - Use of *static routing*, the source and destination of the tunneled networks are declared in the policy and don't need to be declared in routing tables.

- Policy-based VPNs must be used in specific scenarios that require them, such as for compatibility with legacy on-premises VPN devices.
  - If defining which IP addresses are behind each tunnel is too cumbersome, route-based gateways can be used.
  - Use a route-based VPN gateway if you need any of the following types of connectivity:
    - Connections between virtual networks
    - Point-to-site connections
    - Multisite connections
    - Coexistence with an Azure ExpressRoute gateway
    - Supports IKEv2
    - Uses any-to-any (wildcard) traffic selectors
    - Can use *dynamic routing protocols*
  - Before you can deploy a VPN gateway, you'll need some Azure and on-premises resources.
    - Virtual network
    - Gateway Subnet.
    - Public IP address.
    - Local network gateway
    - Virtual network gateway
    - Connection
  - To connect your datacenter to a VPN gateway, you'll need these on-premises resources:
    - A VPN device that supports policy-based or route-based VPN gateways
    - A public-facing (internet-routable) IPv4 address

- In regions that support availability zones, VPN gateways and ExpressRoute gateways can be deployed in a **zone-redundant** configuration.
- This configuration brings resiliency, scalability, and higher availability to virtual network gateways.
- **ExpressRoute failover** is another high-availability option is to configure a VPN gateway as a secure failover path for ExpressRoute connections.
- But **ExpressRoute** aren't immune to physical problems that affect the cables delivering connectivity or outages that affect the complete ExpressRoute location
- A **site-to-site virtual private network isn't an ExpressRoute model**
- ExpressRoute does provide private connectivity, but it **isn't encrypted**.
- ExpressRoute uses the Border Gateway Protocol (BGP) routing protocol.
- BGP protocol enables dynamic routing between your on-premises network and services running in the Microsoft cloud.
- **Features and benefits of ExpressRoute**
  - There are several benefits to using ExpressRoute as the connection service between Azure and on-premises networks.
  - Layer 3 (Network Layer) connectivity between your on-premises network and the Microsoft Cloud through a connectivity provider. Connectivity can be from an any-to-any (IPVPN) network, a point-to-point

Ethernet connection, or through a virtual cross-connection via an Ethernet exchange.

- Connectivity to Microsoft cloud services across all regions in the geopolitical region.
- Global connectivity to Microsoft services across all regions with the ExpressRoute premium add-on.
- Dynamic routing between your network and Microsoft via BGP.
- Built-in redundancy in every peering location for higher reliability.
- Connection uptime SLA.
- QoS support for Skype for Business.

○ ExpressRoute supports three models that you can use to connect your on-premises network to the Microsoft cloud:

- **Cloud Exchange colocation**: Colocated providers can normally offer both Layer 2 and Layer 3 connections between your infrastructures
- **Point-to-point Ethernet connection:** Point-to-point connections provide Layer 2 and Layer 3 connectivity between your on-premises site and Azure.
- **Any-to-any connection:** With any-to-any connectivity, you can integrate your wide area network (WAN) with Azure by providing connections to your offices and datacenters

Azure Storage services

- **Azure Storage account fundamentals**
  - Azure Storage is also used by infrastructure as a service virtual machines, and platform as a service cloud services.
  - To begin using Azure Storage, you first create an Azure Storage account to store your data objects.
  - You can create an Azure Storage account by using the Azure portal, PowerShell, or the Azure CLI.
  - Data in an Azure Storage account is **always replicated three times** in the primary region.
  - Azure Storage offers two options for how your data is replicated in the primary region:
    - **Locally redundant storage (LRS)** copies your data synchronously three times within a single physical location in the primary region. LRS is the least expensive replication option but is not recommended for applications requiring high availability or durability.
    - **Zone-redundant storage (ZRS)** copies your data synchronously across three Azure availability zones in the **primary region**. For applications requiring high availability, Microsoft recommends using ZRS in the primary region, and also replicating to a secondary region.
  - For applications requiring high durability, you can choose to additionally copy the data in your storage account to a secondary region that is hundreds of miles away from the primary region.

- Azure Storage offers two options for copying your data to a secondary region:
    - **Geo-redundant storage (GRS)** copies your data synchronously three times within a single physical location in the primary region using LRS. It then copies your data asynchronously to a single physical location in the secondary region. Within the secondary region, your data is copied synchronously three times using LRS.
    - **Geo-zone-redundant storage (GZRS)** copies your data synchronously across three Azure availability zones in the primary region using ZRS. It then copies your data asynchronously to a single physical location in the secondary region. Within the secondary region, your data is copied synchronously three times using LRS.

- **Disk storage fundamentals**
    - **Azure VMs use Azure Disk Storage to store virtual disks.** However, you **can't use** Azure Disk Storage to store a disk **outside of a virtual machine**.
    - Disk Storage provides disks for Azure virtual machines
    - Disk Storage allows data to be persistently stored and accessed from an attached virtual hard disk.
    - Disks come in many different sizes and performance levels, from solid-state drives (SSDs) to traditional spinning hard disk drives (HDDs), with varying performance tiers.

- **Azure Blob storage**
  - Azure Blob Storage is an object storage solution for the cloud.
  - It can store massive amounts of data, such as text or binary data.
  - Azure Blob Storage is unstructured, meaning that there are no restrictions on the kinds of data it can hold.
  - Blobs aren't limited to common file formats.
  - You store blobs in containers, which helps you organize your blobs depending on your business needs.
  - Blob storage offers three types of resources:
    - The **storage account**
    - A **container** in the storage account
    - A **blob** in a container
  - Blob Storage is ideal for:
    - Serving images or documents directly to a browser.
    - Storing **files for distributed access**.
    - Streaming video and audio.
    - **Storing data for backup and restore, disaster recovery, and archiving.**
    - Storing data for analysis by an on-premises or Azure-hosted service.
    - Storing up to 8 TB of data for virtual machines
  - Azure Storage supports three types of blobs:
    - **Block blobs** store text and binary data. Block blobs are made up of blocks of data that can

be managed individually. Block blobs can store up to about 190.7 TiB.

- **Append blobs** are made up of blocks like block blobs but are optimized for append operations. Append blobs are ideal for scenarios such as logging data from virtual machines.
- **Page blobs** store random access files up to 8 TiB in size. Page blobs store virtual hard drive (VHD) files and serve as disks for Azure virtual machines.

- **Blob access tiers**
  - Azure Storage offers different access tiers for your blob storage, helping you store object data in the most cost-effective manner. The available access tiers include:
    - **Hot access tier**: Optimized for storing data that is accessed frequently (for example, images for your website).
    - **Cool access tier**: Optimized for data that is infrequently accessed and stored for at least 30 days (for example, invoices for your customers).
    - **Archive access tier**: Appropriate for data that is rarely accessed and stored for at least 180 days, with flexible latency requirements (for example, long-term backups).
  - Only the hot and cool access tiers can be set at the account level. The archive access tier isn't available at the account level.

- Hot, cool, and archive tiers can be set at the blob level, during upload or after upload.
- Data in the cool access tier can tolerate slightly lower availability, but still requires high durability, retrieval latency, and throughput characteristics similar to hot data. For cool data, a slightly lower availability service-level agreement (SLA) and **higher access costs compared to hot data** are acceptable trade-offs for **lower storage costs.**
- Archive storage stores data offline and offers **the lowest storage costs**, but also the **highest costs to rehydrate and access data**.

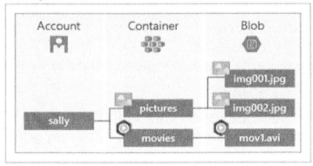

- **Azure Files**
  - Azure Files offers fully managed file shares in the cloud that are accessible via the industry standard Server Message Block and Network File System (preview) protocols.
  - Any number of Azure virtual machines or roles can mount and access the file storage share simultaneously.
  - One thing that distinguishes Azure Files from files on a corporate file share is that you can access the

files from anywhere in the world, by using a URL that points to the file.

- ○ You can also use Shared Access Signature (SAS) tokens to allow access to a private asset for a specific amount of time.
- ○ Use Azure Files for the following situations:
- ○ Many on-premises applications use file shares.
  - ■ Store configuration files on a file share and access them from multiple VMs.
  - ■ Write data to a file share, and process or analyze the data later

- **Azure Table Storage**
  - ○ A NoSQL store for schemaless storage of structured data.
  - ○ Azure Table storage is a service that stores non-relational structured data (also known as structured NoSQL data).
  - ○ Access to Table storage data is fast and cost-effective for many types of applications and is typically lower in cost than traditional SQL for similar volumes of data.
  - ○ You can use Table storage to store flexible datasets like user data for web applications, address books, device information, or other types of metadata your service requires.
  - ○ Common uses of Table storage include:
    - ■ Storing **TBs of structured data** capable of serving web scale applications
    - ■ Storing **datasets that don't require complex joins**, foreign keys, or stored procedures and can be denormalized for fast access.

- **Quickly querying** data using a clustered index.
- **Accessing data using the OData protocol and LINQ queries** with WCF Data Service .NET Libraries.

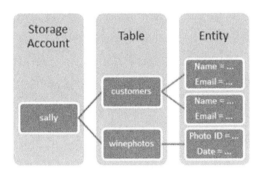

- **Azure Queue**
  - A messaging store for reliable messaging between application components.
  - Azure Queue Storage is a service for storing large numbers of messages.
  - Queues are commonly used to create a backlog of work to process asynchronously.
  - A queue message can be up to 64 KB in size.
  - The queue name **must** be all lowercase.
  - The default **time-to-live of messages** in the queue is **seven days**.

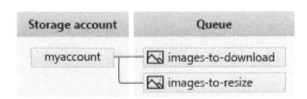

Explore Azure database and analytics services

- **Azure Cosmos DB**
  - Azure Cosmos DB is a globally distributed, **multi-model database service**.
  - Azure Cosmos DB supports **schema-less data**, which lets you build highly responsive and "Always On" applications to support constantly changing data.
  - Azure Cosmos DB stores data in **atom-record-sequence (ARS)** format.
  - **Azure Cosmos DB supports SQL, MongoDB, Cassandra, Tables, and Gremlin APIs.**
  - **When to use:** When your application needs document, table, or graph databases, including MongoDB databases, with multiple well-defined consistency models.

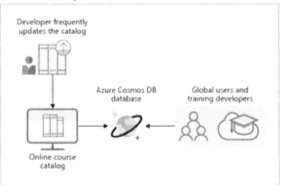

- **Azure SQL Database**
  - Azure SQL Database is a **relational database** based on the latest stable version of the Microsoft **SQL Server database engine**.

- Azure SQL Database is a **platform as a service** (PaaS) database engine.
- SQL Database provides **99.99** percent availability
- Microsoft handles all updates to the SQL and operating system code
- You get the newest SQL Server capabilities, with no overhead for updates or upgrades
- **99.99 - 99.995% availability** is guaranteed for every database.
- **When to use**: When your application requires data storage with referential integrity, transactional support, and support for TSQL queries.

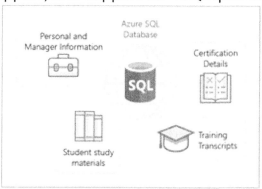

- **Azure Database for MySQL delivers**
  - Built-in high availability with no additional cost.
  - Predictable performance and inclusive, pay-as-you-go pricing.
  - Scale as needed, within seconds.
  - Ability to protect sensitive data at-rest and in-motion.
  - Automatic backups.
  - Enterprise-grade security and compliance.

- Azure Database for MySQL is the logical choice for existing LAMP stack applications.

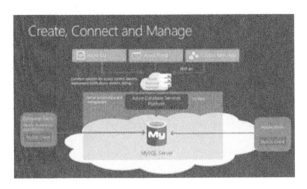

- **Azure Database for PostgreSQL**
  - Built-in high availability compared to on-premises resources.
  - Simple and flexible pricing.
  - Scale up or down as needed, within seconds.
  - Adjustable automatic backups and point-in-time-restore for up to 35 days.
  - Enterprise-grade security and compliance to protect sensitive data at-rest and in-motion.
  - Azure Database for PostgreSQL is available in two deployment options: **Single Server** and **Hyperscale (Citus)**.
  - **Single Server**
    - Built-in high availability with no additional cost (99.99 percent SLA).
    - Predictable performance and inclusive, pay-as-you-go pricing.
    - Vertical scale as needed, within seconds.
    - Monitoring and alerting to assess your server
    - Enterprise-grade security and compliance.

- Ability to protect sensitive data at-rest and in-motion.
- Automatic backups and point-in-time-restore for up to 35 days.
  - **Hyperscale (Citus)**
    - The Hyperscale (Citus) option horizontally scales queries across multiple machines by using sharding.
    - Its query engine parallelizes incoming SQL queries across these servers for faster responses on large datasets.
    - It serves applications that require greater scale and performance,
    - The Hyperscale (Citus) deployment option supports multi-tenant applications, real-time operational analytics, and high throughput transactional workloads.

- **Azure SQL Managed Instance**
  - Azure SQL Managed Instance is a platform as a service (PaaS) database engine.
  - **99.99**.% availability is guaranteed for every database and can't be managed by the user.
  - Azure SQL Managed Instance provides several options that might not be available to Azure SQL Database.
  - Azure SQL Managed Instance makes it easy to migrate your on-premises data on SQL Server to the cloud using the Azure Database Migration Service (DMS) or native backup and restore.

- **Big data and analytics**

- Azure Synapse Analytics:
  - (formerly Azure SQL Data Warehouse) is a limitless analytics service that brings together enterprise data warehousing and big data analytics.
  - Azure Synapse Analytics is the **logical choice for analyzing large volumes** of data.
- Azure HDInsightl
  - t is a fully managed, open-source analytics service for enterprises.
  - It's a cloud service that makes it easier, faster, and more cost-effective to process massive amounts of data.
  - You can run popular open-source frameworks and create cluster types such as Apache Spark, Apache Hadoop, Apache Kafka, Apache HBase, Apache Storm, and Machine Learning Services.
  - **HDInsight** also supports a broad range of scenarios such as extraction, transformation, and loading (ETL), data warehousing, machine learning, and IoT.
- **Azure Databricks**
  - It helps you unlock insights from all your data and build artificial intelligence solutions.
  - You can set up your Apache Spark environment in minutes, and then autoscale and collaborate on shared projects in an interactive workspace
- **Azure Data Lake Analytics**

- It is an on-demand analytics job service that simplifies big data.
- Instead of deploying, configuring, and tuning hardware, you write queries to transform your data and extract valuable insights.

If You Want	Use This
Limitless analytics service with unmatched time to insight	**Azure Synapse Analytics**
A fully managed, fast, easy, and collaborative Apache® Spark™ based analytics platform optimized for Azure	**Azure Databricks**
A fully managed cloud Hadoop and Spark service backed by 99.9% SLA for your enterprise	**HDInsight**
A data integration service to orchestrate and automate data movement and transformation	Azure Data Factory
Open and elastic AI development spanning the cloud and the edge	**Machine Learning**
Real-time data stream processing from millions of IoT devices	Azure Stream Analytics
A fully managed on-demand pay-per-job analytics service with enterprise-grade security, auditing and support	**Data Lake Analytics**
Enterprise-grade analytics engine as a service	Azure Analysis Services
A hyper-scale telemetry ingestion service that collects, transforms and stores millions of events	Event Hubs

Fast and highly scalable data exploration service	Azure Data Explorer
A simple and safe service for sharing big data with external organizations	Azure Data Share
End-to-end IoT analytics platform to monitor, analyze and visualize your industrial IoT data at scale	Azure Time Series Insights
A secure, high-throughput connector designed to copy selected Microsoft 365 productivity datasets into your Azure tenant	Microsoft Graph Data Connect

Core Solutions And Management Tools On Azure

Choose the best AI service for your needs

- **Azure Machine Learning**
  - It is a platform for making predictions.
  - It consists of tools and services that allow you to connect to data to train and test models to find one that will most accurately predict a future result.
  - Choose Azure Machine Learning when your data scientists need complete control over the design and training of an algorithm using your own data.
  - **With Azure Machine Learning, you can:**
    - Create a process that defines how to obtain data, how to handle missing or bad data, how to split the data into either a training set or test set and deliver the data to the training process.
    - Train and evaluate predictive models by using tools and programming languages familiar to data scientists.
    - Create pipelines that define where and when to run the compute-intensive experiments that are required to score the algorithms based on the training and test data.
    - Deploy the best-performing algorithm as an API to an endpoint so it can be consumed in real time by other applications.
    - Choose Azure Machine Learning when you need to analyze data to predict future outcomes.

- **Azure Cognitive Services**

- provides prebuilt machine learning models that enable applications to see, hear, speak, understand, and even begin to reason.
- Use Azure Cognitive Services when it comes to general purpose tasks, such as performing speech to text, integrating with search, or identifying the objects in an image.
- You don't need special machine learning or data science knowledge to use these services.
- Azure Cognitive Services can be divided into the following categories:
  - **Language** services
  - **Speech** services
  - **Vision** services
  - **Decision** services

- **Azure Bot Service**
  - Azure Bot Service and Bot Framework are platforms for creating virtual agents that understand and reply to questions just like a human.
  - Azure Bot Service is a bit different from Azure Machine Learning and Azure Cognitive Services in that it has a specific use case.
  - Bots can be used to shift simple, repetitive tasks.
  - A bot interaction can be a quick question and answer, or it can be a sophisticated conversation that intelligently provides access to services.

Choose the best Azure IoT Service for your Application

- **Azure IoT Hub:**
  - It is a managed service that's hosted in the cloud and that acts as a central message hub for bi-directional communication between your IoT application and the devices it manages.
  - IoT Hub allows for command and control

- **Azure IoT Central**
  - builds on top of IoT Hub by adding a dashboard that allows you to connect, monitor, and manage your IoT devices.
  - allows you to push a software update or modify a property of the device.
  - A key part of IoT Central is the use of device templates. By using a device template, you can connect a device without any service-side coding.
  - IoT Central quickly creates a web-based management portal to enable reporting and communication with IoT devices.

- **Azure Sphere**
  - creates an end-to-end, highly secure IoT solution for customers.
  - Azure Sphere provides a complete solution for scenarios where security is critical.
  - Azure Sphere comes in three parts:
    - The first part is the Azure Sphere micro-controller unit (MCU), which is

responsible for processing the operating system and signals from attached sensors.

- The second part is a customized Linux operating system (OS) that handles communication with the security service and can run the vendor's software.
- The third part is Azure Sphere Security Service, also known as AS3. Its job is to make sure that the device has not been maliciously compromised

Tools to help organizations build better solutions

- **Azure DevOps Services**
  - It is a SaaS.
  - Azure DevOps Services is a suite of services that address every stage of the software development lifecycle.
    - **Azure Repos** is a centralized source-code repository where software development, DevOps engineering, and documentation professionals can publish their code for review and collaboration.
    - **Azure Boards** is an agile project management suite that includes Kanban boards, reporting, and tracking ideas and work from high-level epics to work items and issues.
    - **Azure Pipelines** is a CI/CD pipeline automation tool.
    - **Azure Artifacts** is a repository for hosting artifacts, such as compiled source code, which can be fed into testing or deployment pipeline steps.
    - **Azure Test Plans** is an automated test tool that can be used in a CI/CD pipeline to ensure quality before a software release.

- **GitHub and GitHub Actions**
  - Git is a decentralized source-code management tool, and GitHub is a hosted version of Git that serves as the primary remote.
  - GitHub builds on top of Git.
  - It offers the following functionality:

- It's a shared source-code repository, including tools that enable developers to perform code reviews by adding comments and questions in a web view of the source code before it can be merged into the main code base.
- It facilitates project management, including Kanban boards.
- It supports issue reporting, discussion, and tracking.
- It features CI/CD pipeline automation tooling.
- It includes a wiki for collaborative documentation.
- It can be run from the cloud or on-premises
  - **GitHub Actions** enables workflow automation with triggers for many lifecycle events
  - GitHub is a lighter-weight tool than Azure DevOps, with a focus on individual developers contributing to the open-source code.
  - Azure DevOps and GitHub allow public and private code repositories.

- **Azure DevTest Labs**
  - Azure DevTest Labs provides an automated means of managing the process of building, setting up, and tearing down virtual machines (VMs) that contain builds of your software projects.
  - Anything you can deploy in Azure via an ARM template can be provisioned through DevTest Labs.
  - Azure DevTest Labs can set up everything automatically upon request.

Tools for managing and configuring your Azure environment

- **The Azure portal**
  - Azure portal, a web-based user interface, you can access virtually every feature of Azure.
  - The Azure portal provides a friendly, graphical UI to view all the services you're using, create new services, configure your services, and view reports.

- **The Azure mobile app**
  - The Azure mobile app provides iOS and Android access to your Azure resources when you're away from your computer.
  - With it, you can:
    - Monitor the health and status of your Azure resources.
    - Check for alerts, quickly diagnose, and fix issues, and restart a web app or virtual machine (VM).
    - Run the Azure CLI or Azure PowerShell commands to manage your Azure resources.

- **Azure PowerShell**
  - Azure PowerShell is a shell with which developers and DevOps and IT professionals can execute commands called cmdlets (pronounced *command-lets*).
  - These commands call the Azure Rest API to perform every possible management task in Azure.

- Cmdlets can be executed independently or combined into a script file and executed together to orchestrate:
  - The routine setup, teardown, and maintenance of a single resource or multiple connected resources.
  - The deployment of an entire infrastructure, which might contain dozens or hundreds of resources, from imperative code.
- Capturing the commands in a script makes the process repeatable and automatable.

- **Azure PowerShell**
  - It is available for Windows, Linux, and Mac, and you can access it in a web browser via Azure Cloud Shell.

- **The Azure CLI**
  - The Azure CLI command-line interface is an executable program with which a developer, DevOps professional, or IT professional can execute commands in Bash.
  - The commands call the Azure Rest API to perform every possible management task in Azure.
  - You can run the commands independently or combined into a script and executed together for the routine setup, teardown, and maintenance of a single resource or an entire environment.
  - The Azure CLI enables you to use Bash to run one-off tasks on Azure.
  - In many respects, the Azure CLI is almost identical to Azure PowerShell in what you can do with it.

- Both run on Windows, Linux, and Mac, and can be accessed in a web browser via Cloud Shell.
- The primary difference is the syntax you use. If you're already proficient in PowerShell or Bash, you can use the tool you prefer.

- **ARM templates**
  - By using Azure Resource Manager templates (ARM templates), you can describe the resources you want to use in a declarative JSON format.
  - The benefit is that the entire ARM template is verified before any code is executed to ensure that the resources will be created and connected correctly.
  - The template then orchestrates the creation of those resources in parallel. That is, if you need 50 instances of the same resource, all 50 instances are created at the same time.
    - Templates can even execute PowerShell and Bash scripts before or after the resource has been set up.
    - ARM templates are the best infrastructure-as-code option for quickly and reliably setting up your entire cloud infrastructure declaratively.
    - **When to use**: Use Resource Manager templates when you want a template-based deployment for your app that you can manage programmatically by using REST APIs, the Azure CLI, and Azure PowerShell.

Monitoring service for visibility, insight, and outage mitigation

- **Azure Advisor**
  - Azure Advisor evaluates your Azure resources and makes recommendations to help improve reliability, security, and performance, achieve operational excellence, and reduce costs.
  - Advisor is designed to help you save time on cloud optimization.
  - The recommendation service includes suggested actions you can take right away, postpone, or dismiss.
  - The recommendations are available via the Azure portal and the API, and you can set up notifications to alert you to new recommendations.
  - The recommendations are divided into five categories:
    - **Reliability**: Used to ensure and improve the continuity of your business-critical applications.
    - **Security**: Used to detect threats and vulnerabilities that might lead to security breaches.
    - **Performance**: Used to improve the speed of your applications.
    - **Cost**: Used to optimize and reduce your overall Azure spending.
    - **Operational Excellence**: Used to help you achieve process and workflow efficiency,

resource manageability, and deployment best practices.

- **Azure Monitor**
  - It is a platform for collecting, analyzing, visualizing, and potentially acting based on the metric and logging data from your entire Azure and on-premises environment.
  - Use Azure Monitor to set up alerts for outages and other events that affect only your specific resources.
  - Application Insights relies on the Azure Monitor platform to store custom event information.

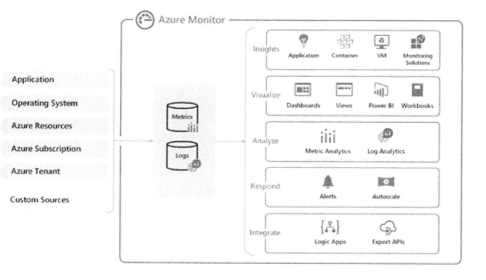

- **Azure Service Health**
  - provides a personalized view of the health of the Azure services, regions, and resources you rely on.
  - The **status.azure.com** website, which displays only major issues that broadly affect Azure customers, doesn't provide the full picture.

- Azure Service Health displays both major and smaller, localized issues that affect you.
- You **can set up alerts** that help you triage outages and planned maintenance.
- After an outage, Service Health provides official incident reports, called **root cause analyses (RCAs),** which you can share with stakeholders
- Service Health helps you keep an eye on several event types:
    - Service issue
    - Planned maintenance
    - Health advisories

General Security And Network Security Features

Protect against security threats on Azure

- **Azure Security Center**
  - **Protect against security threats by using Azure Security Center**
  - It is a **monitoring service** that provides visibility of your security posture across all your services, both on Azure and on-premises.
  - With Azure Security Center, you can define a list of allowed applications to ensure that only applications you allow can run.
  - Azure Security Center can also detect and block malware from being installed on your VMs.
  - **Monitor security settings** across on-premises and cloud workloads.
  - **Automatically apply required security settings** to new resources as they come online.
  - **Provide security recommendations** that are based on your current configurations, resources, and networks.
  - Continuously **monitor your resources** and perform automatic security assessments to identify potential vulnerabilities before those vulnerabilities can be exploited.
  - Use machine learning to **detect and block malware** from being installed on your virtual machines (VMs) and other resources.
  - **Detect and analyze potential inbound attacks** and investigate threats and any post-breach activity that might have occurred.

- ○ **Provide just-in-time access control** for network ports. Doing so reduces your attack surface by ensuring that the network only allows traffic that you require at the time that you need it to.
- ○ Secure score is a measurement of an organization's security posture.
- ○ The term *security posture* **refers** to cybersecurity policies and controls, as well as how well you can predict, prevent, and respond to security threats.
- ○ The common principles used to define a security posture are *confidentiality*, *integrity*, **and** *availability*, known collectively as CIA.
- ○ Secure score is based on *security controls*, or groups of related security recommendations.
- ○ Security Center includes advanced cloud defense capabilities for VMs, network security, and file integrity like:
  - ■ Just-in-time VM access
  - ■ Adaptive application controls
  - ■ Adaptive network hardening
  - ■ File integrity monitoring

- **Azure Sentinel**
  - ○ Detect and respond to security threats by using Azure Sentinel
  - ○ It is Microsoft's cloud-based **security information and event management** (SIEM) system. It uses intelligent **security analytics and threat analysis**.
  - ○ A SIEM aggregates security data from many different sources to provide additional capabilities for threat detection and responding to threats.

- It has both built-in analytics and custom rules to detect threats.
- Azur Sentinel Capabilities:
  - Collect cloud data at scale
  - Detect previously undetected threats
  - Investigate threats with artificial intelligence
  - Respond to incidents rapidly

- **Azure Key Vault**
  - It is a centralized cloud service for storing an application's secrets in a single, central location.
  - It provides secure access to sensitive information by providing access control and logging capabilities.
  - The benefits of using Key Vault include:
    - Centralized application secrets
    - Securely stored secrets and keys
    - Access monitoring and access control
    - Simplified administration of application secrets
    - Integration with other Azure services
  - Azure Key Vault can help you:
    - Manage secrets
    - Manage encryption keys
    - Manage SSL/TLS certificates
    - Store secrets backed by hardware security modules (HSMs)

Search (Ctrl+/)   + Generate/Import   ⟳ Refresh   ↑ Restore Backup   ✉ Certificate Contacts

① Overview

⊟ Activity log   Name   Thumbprint   Status

ጸ Access control (IAM)   Completed

❀ Tags   TestCACert   88D24EFCF38AE6ACDA8B...   ✓ Enabled

🔗 Diagnose and solve problems   In progress, failed or cancelled

⚡ Events (preview)   There are no certificates available.

- **Azur Dedicated Host**
  - Provides dedicated physical servers to host your Azure VMs for Windows and Linux.
  - A *dedicated host* is mapped to a physical server in an Azure datacenter. A *host group* is a collection of dedicated hosts.
  - Gives you visibility into, and control over, the server infrastructure that's running your Azure VMs.
  - Helps address compliance requirements by deploying your workloads on an isolated server.
  - Let's choose the number of processors, server capabilities, VM series, and VM sizes within the same host.
  - You're charged per dedicated host, independent of how many VMs you deploy to it. The host price is based on the VM family, type (hardware size), and region.

  - Software licensing, storage, and network usage are billed separately from the host and VMs.

Host group

- Name
- Region
- Optional:
Availability zone
and fault domain
count

Dedicated host

- Name
- Asset ID
- Fault domain
- SKU

Virtual machines

- Name
- ID
- Size

7

Secure network connectivity on Azure

- **Defense in Depth**
  - The *physical security* **layer** is the first line of defense to **protect computing hardware** in the datacenter.
  - The *identity and access* **layer** controls access to infrastructure and change control. Use single sign-on (SSO) and multifactor authentication.
  - The *perimeter* **layer** uses distributed denial of service **(DDoS) protection** to filter large-scale attacks before they can cause a denial of service for users. Firewall is part of the perimeter security
  - The *network* **layer** *limits communication* between resources through segmentation and access controls. limiting connectivity to and from specific devices or subnets within a virtual network
  - The *compute* **layer secures access to virtual machines**. Implement endpoint protection on devices
  - The *application* **layer** helps ensure that applications are **secure and free of security vulnerabilities.**
  - The *data* **layer controls access** to business and customer data that you need to protect.

- **Azure Firewall**
  - A *firewall* is a network security device that monitors incoming and outgoing network traffic and decides whether to allow or block specific traffic based on a defined set of security rules.

- It is a managed, cloud-based network security service that helps protect resources in your Azure virtual networks.
- Azure Firewall enables you to limit outbound HTTP/S traffic to a specified list of fully qualified domain names (FQDNs).
- It's a fundamental building block for your private network.
- Azure Firewall is a *stateful* firewall. A stateful firewall analyzes the complete context of a network connection, not just an individual packet of network traffic.
- Azure Firewall provides many features, including:
    - Built-in high availability.
    - Unrestricted cloud scalability.
    - Inbound and outbound filtering rules.
    - Inbound Destination Network Address Translation (DNAT) support.
    - Azure Monitor logging.
- You typically deploy Azure Firewall on a central virtual network to control general network access.

- **Azure DDoS Protection**
    - helps protect your Azure resources from DDoS attacks
    - DDoS Protection can also help you manage your cloud consumption.
    - The Basic service tier is automatically enabled for free as part of your Azure subscription.
    - The Standard service tier can help prevent:
        - **Volumetric attacks**
        - **Protocol attacks**

- Resource-layer (application-layer) attacks (only with web application firewall)

- **Network Security Group**
  - It enables you to filter network traffic to and from Azure resources within an Azure virtual network.
  - You can think of NSGs like an internal firewall.
  - A network security group rule enables you to filter traffic to and from resources by source and destination IP address, port, and protocol.
  - Network Security Group (NSG) - a fairly basic set of rules that you can apply to both inbound traffic and outbound traffic that lets you specify what sources, destinations and ports are allowed to travel through from outside the virtual network to inside the virtual network
  - An NSG can contain multiple inbound and outbound security rules that enable you to filter traffic to and from resources by source and destination IP address, port, and protocol.
  - When you create a network security group, Azure creates a series of default rules to provide a baseline level of security. You can't remove the default rules, but you can override them by creating new rules with higher priorities.

Identity, Governance, Privacy, And Compliance Features

Secure access to your applications by using Azure identity services

- **Authentication and Authorization**
  - Authentication is the process of establishing the identity of a person or service that wants to access a resource.
  - Authentication establishes the user's identity, but authorization is the process of establishing what level of access an authenticated person or service has.
- **Azure Active Directory (Azure AD)**
  - Azure Active Directory (Azure AD) provides identity services that enable your users to sign in and access both Microsoft cloud applications and cloud applications that you develop.
  - Active Directory is related to Azure AD, but they have some key differences.
  - Azure Active Directory provides the following licenses: **Free, "Pay as you go", Premium P1, and Premium P2.**
  - With Azure AD, you control the identity accounts, but Microsoft ensures that the service is available globally.
  - When you connect Active Directory with Azure AD, Microsoft can help protect you by detecting suspicious sign-in attempts at no extra cost.
  - When you secure identities on-premises with Active Directory, Microsoft doesn't monitor sign-in attempts.

- Microsoft 365, Microsoft Office 365, Azure, and Microsoft Dynamics CRM Online subscribers are already using Azure AD
- A tenant is a representation of an organization. **A tenant is typically separated from other tenants and has its own identity.**
- Each Microsoft 365, Office 365, Azure, and Dynamics CRM **Online tenant is automatically an Azure AD tenant.**
- **Azure tenant** is a dedicated and trusted instance of Azure AD that's automatically created when your organization signs up for a Microsoft cloud service subscription, such as Microsoft Azure, Microsoft Intune, or Microsoft 365. An Azure tenant represents a single organization.
- Azure tenants that access other services in a dedicated environment are considered **single tenant**.
- Azure tenants that access other services in a shared environment, across multiple organizations, are considered **multi-tenant**.
- Azure AD is for:
  - IT administrators
  - App developers
  - Users
  - Online service subscribers
- Azure AD provides services such as:
  - Authentication
  - Single sign-on
  - Application management
  - Device management

- **Multi Factor authentication**
  - It is a process where a user is prompted during the sign-in process for an additional form of identification. Examples include a code on their mobile phone or a fingerprint scan.
  - **Conditional Access** is a tool that Azure Active Directory uses to allow (or deny) access to resources based on identity *signals*.
  - Conditional Access enables you to require users to access your applications only from approved, or managed, devices.
  - Conditional Access comes with a *What If* tool, which helps you plan and troubleshoot your Conditional Access policies.
  - Conditional Access helps IT administrators:
    - Empower users to be productive wherever and whenever.
    - Protect the organization's assets.
  - Conditional Access also provides a more granular multifactor authentication experience for users.
  - To use Conditional Access, you need an Azure AD Premium P1 or P2 license. If you have a Microsoft 365 Business Premium license, you also have access to Conditional Access features.
  - Multifactor authentication provides additional security for your identities by requiring two or more elements to fully authenticate.
  - These elements fall into three categories:
    - **Something the user knows:** This might be an email address and password.

- **Something the user has:** This might be a code that's sent to the user's mobile phone.
- **Something the user is:** This is typically some sort of biometric property, such as a fingerprint or face scan that's used on many mobile devices.

Build a cloud governance strategy on Azure

- **Azure Role-based access control (RBAC)**
  - Azure provides built-in roles that describe common access rules for cloud resources.
  - Role-based access control is applied to a *scope*, which is a resource or set of resources that this access applies to.
  - Scopes include:
    - A management group (a collection of multiple subscriptions).
    - A single subscription.
    - A resource group.
    - A single resource.
  - When you grant access at a parent scope, those permissions are inherited by all child scopes.
  - Azure RBAC is enforced on any action that's initiated against an Azure resource that passes through Azure Resource Manager.
  - Azure RBAC enables you to create roles that define access permissions. You might create one role that limits access only to virtual machines and a second role that provides administrators with access to everything.
  - RBAC uses an *allow model*. When you're assigned a role, RBAC *allows* you to perform certain actions, such as read, write, or delete.
  - If one role assignment grants you read permissions to a resource group and a different role assignment grants you write permissions to the same resource

group, you have both read and write permissions on that resource group.
- You can apply Azure RBAC to an individual person or to a group. You can also apply Azure RBAC to other special identity types, such as service principals and managed identities.

- **Resource Lock**
  - A resource lock prevents resources from being accidentally deleted or changed.
  - You can manage resource locks from the *Azure portal, PowerShell, the Azure CLI, or from an Azure Resource Manager template*.
  - You can apply locks to a subscription, a resource group, or an individual resource. You can set the lock level to **CanNotDelete** or **ReadOnly**.
  - **CanNotDelete** means authorized people *can still read and modify a resource*, but they can't *delete the resource without first removing the lock*.
  - **ReadOnly** means authorized people can read a resource, but they can't delete or change the resource. Applying this lock is like restricting all authorized users to the permissions granted by the **Reader** role in Azure RBAC.
  - Resource locks apply regardless of RBAC permissions

- **Tags**
  - Tags provide extra information, or metadata, about your resources.
  - This metadata is useful for:

- **Resource management:** Tags enable you to locate and act on resources that are associated with specific workloads, environments, business units, and owners.
- **Security:** Tags enable you to classify data by its security level, such as *public* or *confidential*.
- **Cost management and optimization:** Tags enable you to group resources so that you can report on costs, allocate internal cost centers, track budgets, and forecast estimated cost.
- **Operations management:** Tags enable you to group resources according to how critical their availability is to your business.
- **Governance and regulatory compliance:** Tags enable you to identify resources that align with governance or regulatory compliance requirements, such as ISO 27001.
- **Workload optimization and automation:** Tags can help you visualize all of the resources that participate in complex deployments.

  - You can add, modify, or delete resource tags through *PowerShell, the Azure CLI, Azure Resource Manager templates, the REST API, or the Azure portal.*

- **Azure Policy**
  - It is a service in Azure that enables you to create, assign, and manage policies that control or audit your resources.

- Azure Policy enables you to define both individual policies and groups of related policies, known as *initiatives*
- Azure Policy can also <u>prevent noncompliant resources from being created</u>.
- Implementing a policy in Azure Policy involves these three steps:
  - Create a policy definition.
  - Assign the definition to resources.
  - Review the evaluation results.
- An **Azure Policy initiative** is a way of grouping related policies into one set.
- The initiative definition contains all of the policy definitions to help track your compliance state for a larger goal.

- **Azure Blueprints**
  - with Azure Blueprints you can define a repeatable set of governance tools and standard Azure resources that your organization requires.
  - Azure Blueprints orchestrates the deployment of various resource templates and other artifacts, such as:
    - Role assignments
    - Policy assignments
    - Azure Resource Manager templates
    - Resource groups
  - Blueprints are also versioned. Versioning enables you to track and comment on changes to your blueprint.

- **Cloud Adoption Framework**

- The Cloud Adoption Framework for Azure provides you with proven guidance to help with your cloud adoption journey.
- The Cloud Adoption Framework helps you create and implement the business and technology strategies needed to succeed in the cloud.
- The Cloud Adoption Framework includes these stages:
  - Define your strategy.
  - Make a plan.
  - Ready your organization.
  - Adopt the cloud.
  - Govern and manage your cloud environments.

Examine privacy, compliance, and data protection standards on Azure

- **Microsoft Privacy Statement**
    - The Microsoft Privacy Statement explains what personal data Microsoft collects, how Microsoft uses it, and for what purposes.
    - The privacy statement covers all of Microsoft's services, websites, apps, software, servers, and devices.
    - The Microsoft Privacy Statement provides information that's relevant to specific services, including Cortana.

- **Online Services Terms**
    - The Online Services Terms (OST) is a legal agreement between Microsoft and the customer.
    - The OST details the obligations by both parties with respect to the processing and security of customer data and personal data.
    - The OST applies specifically to Microsoft's online services that you license through a subscription, including Azure, Dynamics 365, Office 365, and Bing Maps.

- **Data Protection Addendum**
    - The Data Protection Addendum (DPA) further defines the data processing and security terms for online services. These terms include:
        - Compliance with laws.
        - Disclosure of processed data.

- Data Security, which includes security practices and policies, data encryption, data access, customer responsibilities, and compliance with auditing.
- Data transfer, retention, and deletion.

- **Trust Center**
  - The Trust Center provides you with documentation about compliance standards and how Azure can support your business.
  - The Trust Center showcases Microsoft's principles for maintaining data integrity in the cloud and how Microsoft implements and supports security, privacy, compliance, and transparency in all Microsoft cloud products and services.
  - The Trust Center is a great resource for people in your organization who might play a role in security, privacy, and compliance.
  - Azure compliance documentation
  - The Azure compliance documentation provides you with detailed documentation about legal and regulatory standards and compliance on Azure.
  - Here you find compliance offerings across these categories:
    - Global
    - US government
    - Financial services
    - Health
    - Media and manufacturing
    - Regional

- **Azure Government**

- It is a separate instance of the Microsoft Azure service.
- It addresses the security and compliance needs of US federal agencies, state and local governments, and their solution providers.
- Azure Government offers physical isolation from non-US government deployments and provides screened US personnel.
- Azure Government customers, such as the US federal, state, and local government or their partners, are subject to validation of eligibility.
- Azure Government provides the broadest compliance and Level 5 DoD approval. Azure Government is available in eight geographies and offers the most compliance certifications of any cloud provider.
- Azure Government services handle data that is subject to certain government regulations and requirements:
  - Federal Risk and Authorization Management Program (FedRAMP)
  - National Institute of Standards and Technology (NIST) 800.171 Defense Industrial Base (DIB)
  - International Traffic in Arms Regulations (ITAR)
  - Internal Revenue Service (IRS) 1075
  - Department of Defense (DoD) L4
  - Criminal Justice Information Service (CJIS)

- The **Azure compliance documentation** includes detailed information about legal and regulatory standards and compliance on Azure.
- The Azure compliance documentation provides you with detailed documentation about legal and regulatory standards and compliance on Azure.
- The compliance documentation provides reference blueprints, or policy definitions, for common standards that you can apply to your Azure subscription.

Azure Cost Management And Service Level Agreements

Plan and manage your Azure costs

- **TCO Calculator**
  - The TCO Calculator helps you estimate the cost savings of operating your solution on Azure over time, instead of in your on-premises datacenter.
  - You don't need an Azure subscription to work with the TCO Calculator.
  - Working with the TCO Calculator involves three steps:
    - Define your workloads.
    - Adjust assumptions.
    - View the report.
- **Purchase services on Azure**
  - Azure offers both free and paid subscription options to fit your needs and requirements. They are:
    - **Free Trial**
    - **Pay-as-you-go**
    - **Member offers**
  - There are three main ways to purchase services on Azure. They are:
    - **Through an Enterprise Agreement**
    - **Directly from the web**
    - **Through a Cloud Solution Provider**
  - The way you use resources, your subscription type, Billing zones, Location, and pricing from third-party vendors are common factors. These factor affect your cost
- **Manage and Minimize your cost**
  - **Azure Advisor** identifies unused or underutilized resources and recommends unused resources that

you can remove. This information helps you configure your resources to match your actual workload.

- Use spending limits to prevent accidental overrun
- **Azure Reservations** offers discounted prices on certain Azure services. Azure Reservations can save you up to **72 percent** as compared to pay-as-you-go prices.
- The cost of Azure products, services, and resources can vary across locations and regions. If possible, you should use them in those locations and regions where they cost less.
- **Azure Cost Management + Billing** is a free service that helps you understand your Azure bill, manage your account and subscriptions, monitor and control Azure spending, and optimize resource use.
- *Tags* help you manage costs associated with the different groups of Azure products and resources. You can apply tags to groups of Azure resources to organize billing data.
- A common recommendation that you'll find from Azure Cost Management + Billing and Azure Advisor is to resize or shut down VMs that are underutilized or idle.
- Recall that to *deallocate* a VM means to no longer run the VM, but preserve the associated hard disks and data in Azure.
- This recommendation might sound obvious, but if you aren't using a resource, you should shut it down.

- If you've purchased licenses for Windows Server or SQL Server, and your licenses are covered by Software Assurance, you might be able to repurpose those licenses on VMs on Azure.

Choose the right Azure services by examining SLAs and service lifecycle

- **Service Level Agreements (SLAs)**
  - Understanding the SLA for each Azure service you use helps you understand what guarantees you can expect.
  - You don't need an Azure subscription to review service SLAs.
  - Each Azure service defines its own SLA.
  - An SLA describes how Microsoft responds when an Azure service fails to perform to its specification.
  - The primary performance commitment typically focuses on uptime, or the percentage of time that a product or service is successfully operational. Some SLAs focus on other factors as well, including latency, or how fast the service must respond to a request.
  - A **service credit** is the percentage of the fees you paid that are credited back to you according to the claim approval process.
  - Credits typically increase as uptime decreases.
  - Typically, you need to file a claim with Microsoft to receive a service credit.
  - Free products typically don't have an SLA.
- **Service lifecycle**
  - The service lifecycle defines how every Azure service is released for public use.
  - Every Azure service starts in the development phase. Next the service is released to the public preview phase.

- After a new Azure service is validated and tested, it's released to all customers as a production-ready service. This is known as general availability (GA).
- Some previews aren't covered by customer support.
- You can access preview features that are specific to the Azure portal from Microsoft Azure (Preview).

Some Other Concepts

- **CDN**
  - **Content Delivery Network** - allows you to improve performance by removing the burden of serving static, unchanging files from the main server to a network of servers around the globe;
  - a CDN can reduce traffic to a server by 50% or more, which means you can serve more users or serve the same users faster; SaaS.
  - A content delivery network (CDN) is a distributed network of servers that can efficiently deliver web content to users.
  - CDNs' store cached content on **edge servers in point-of-presence (POP) locations** that are close to end users, to minimize latency.
  - To use Azure CDN, you must own at least one Azure subscription. You also need to create at least one CDN profile, which is a collection of CDN endpoints.
  - Each Azure subscription has default limits for the following resources:
    - The number of CDN profiles that can be created.
    - The number of endpoints that can be created in a CDN profile.
    - The number of custom domains that can be mapped to an endpoint.
  - Azure CDN offers the following key features:
    - Dynamic site acceleration
    - CDN caching rules
    - HTTPS custom domain support
    - Azure diagnostics logs
    - File compression

- Geo-filtering
- Caching can occur at multiple levels between the origin server and the end user:
  - **Web server**: Uses a shared cache (for multiple users).
  - **Content delivery network**: Uses a shared cache (for multiple users).
  - **Internet service provider (ISP)**: Uses a shared cache (for multiple users).
  - **Web browser**: Uses a private cache (for one user).
- **Azure Cache for Redis**
  - Azure Cache for Redis provides an in-memory data store based on the Redis software.
  - Redis improves the performance and scalability of an application that uses backend data stores heavily.
  - It's able to process large volumes of application requests by keeping frequently accessed data in the server memory, which can be written to and read from quickly.
  - Redis brings a critical low-latency and high-throughput data storage solution to modern applications.
  - Azure Cache for Redis can be used as a distributed data or content cache, a session store, a message broker, and more.
  - Azure Cache for Redis offers both the Redis open-source (OSS Redis) and a commercial product from Redis Labs (Redis Enterprise) as a managed service.

- It can be deployed as a standalone. Or, it can be deployed along with other Azure database services, such as Azure SQL or Cosmos DB.
- Azure Cache for Redis is available in these tiers: *Basic, Standard, Premium, Enterprise, Enterprise Flash*

- **Azure Microservices:**
  - **Azure Service Fabric** is a **distributed systems** platform. This platform makes it easy to build, package, deploy, and manage scalable and reliable microservices
  - **When to use:** Service Fabric is a good choice when you're creating an application or rewriting an existing application to use a microservice architecture.
  - Use Service Fabric when you need more control over, or direct access to, the underlying infrastructure.
  - **Azure Spring Cloud** is a **serverless microservices** platform that enables you to build, deploy, scale and monitor your applications in the cloud.
  - **When to use:** As a fully managed service Azure Spring Cloud is a good choice when you're minimizing operational cost running Spring Boot/Spring Cloud based microservices on Azure.

- **References:**
  - https://docs.microsoft.com/en-us/azure
  - https://docs.microsoft.com/en-gb/learn/certificatio ns/azure-fundamentals/

- **For Practice Questions:**

- https://singhak.in/az-900-practice-question/

Printed in Great Britain
by Amazon

78916175R00061